MOTH

VIP

ER

ER

Attention schools and businesses: for discounted copies on large orders, please contact the publisher directly.

For information contact:

Unsolicited Press

Portland, Oregon

www.unsolicitedpress.com

orders@unsolicitedpress.com

619-354-8005

Cover Design: Kathryn Gerhardt

Editor: Summer Stewart

ISBN: 978-1-963115-45-1

"Your absence has gone through me
Like thread through a needle.
Everything I do is stitched with its color."
—W.S. Merwin

"I thought: I cannot bear this world a moment longer.
  Then, child, make another."
—Madeline Miller, *Circe*

Table of Contents

III. ALMOST MOTHER

ASK ORPHEUS, ASK LOT'S WIFE

it's a sin to look back. on burnt cities, on deepest love.
      to tread worn paths, to relish reruns.
learn from history or repeat it, but always keep
      your eyes ahead. let the sun go down on what
we were, be enamored with what is.

we're in it now, my love. the underworld behind, hope
      ahead—how can I not look to you, oh starlight?
rue or rejoice, how can you ask me not to watch
      my old life burn? all gods are tyrants, fashioned
in their creator's image. my body turns on its axis,
      yesterday and tomorrow trapped in peripheral.

I. MISSOURI GIRL

The Moths

My grandmother collected
moths that loitered around
her back-porch light, stored

them in an old shoebox
in the pantry. I sat coloring
at the kitchen table, heard

the rustle of brown and gray
wings behind the closed door,
the growing panic of a trapped

creature. To this day, I can
think of no earthly reason why
my grandmother would catch

and slowly murder moths
in a cardboard casket.
Must have been a dream—

one of those night images
that clung to me as a child
until it took on the haunting

sheen of memory. She baked
sugar cookies and apple pies,
let six-year-old me name

her dog, paste cartoon stickers
to her vanity mirror. But
for the life of me, I keep

remembering those goddamn
moths, the desperate flutter
only slightly worse than
the silence that followed.

Echoes

measure night's passage in headlight rectangles // I am not who I thought I would be / and yet / I know myself now / a way I didn't then / an intimacy I didn't realize I lacked // in the mirror / I touch my face / lean forward until gold / flecks shimmer in my eyes / another, distant galaxy // *green* the highway patrol officer called them / the one who passed me on my second driver's test / glancing up in a quiet Friday office // *hazel* the word my mother used / pair of jewels she gave me / credit due // my gray-eyed sibling / too close in temper and shape / to be foundling / although I'm sure they dream of it / not belonging to any of us // when they were born / my grandmother bought me a lion shirt / the only time she gave me / a thing I asked for // I wore it to the hospital / bewildered by the wide-eyed creature / in my arms // we still perplex one another / but we are too much the same / cut whole-cloth from two people / who don't like the things / we turned out to be // twenty years from now / I can't say where and who we will become / but they will call / and I will answer.

Displaced

In the front yard stood a big tree—old, broad, solid.
          They didn't tear it down. This is not
      that kind of story. It's probably still
there, looking out over the street,
          but I am not. This is that kind of story.

There are keys on my metal ring
          that open doors I haven't seen
      in years. Likely all the locks
have changed, and I own keys
          that open nothing.

I once said the hardest thing
          I'd ever done was delete a dead man
      from my phone.

On the elementary school playground,
          we picked yellow dandelions, rubbed petals
      inside each other's arms, called the marks
pee stains. A joke no one laughed at, tired
          before it was even told.

Urban Folklore

I learned a different language, hints of frail
heritage my mother clung to in a little white

house on the wrong side of the tracks. Reading
rain in inside-out leaves on trees, storm in pale

red shift of sky, wishes on upturned hems. Beliefs
I thought universal until I voiced them aloud.

No country wisdom for either side of my family,
town people both, but still whimsical drips, inherited

weather-predicting and ghost stories, passed down
from grandmother to mother to me. A recluse witch

who lived across the street, healed my aunt's burnt
hands as a toddler. A dead man knocking at the window,

politely bringing news. This lore was all I had to feel
mysterious, to convince myself I was someone

who saw hidden things, had a third eye and sixth
sense, heard whispers late at night from shadows

running along the wall. We all just want to be special,
something striking, something more. And I wanted

to look death in the eye, to feel haunted in daylight,
because then I wouldn't feel so very much alone.

June Burial

She was the center that couldn't hold,
frozen in sepia, never quite in color.
Lived too long, knew too many ghosts.

They took to knocking on windows
most nights, muttering about caught fish.
She thought to follow them, but it took

her years to find the path beneath the stars,
where the moon held water and cicadas
screamed to the black sky. At the funeral

her smug daughter-in-law pronounced her
a last-minute Republican convert,
as though that secured her ticket to heaven.

It was hot in the cemetery, counting
my relatives among the rows and watching
her lavender casket descend—

the box she'd chosen decades before.
Among the flowers stood the arrangement
my in-laws had sent. I didn't take it

home, although my aunt asked me to.
I didn't want a keepsake, another thing
to look after, on top of two cats and a dog,

a rental house on a cul-de-sac full of windows
missing screens the landlord months
before had promised to finally replace.

The Girl at the End of the Street

Her white-gold hair, the house down the hill
      from mine. We shared a bus stop and later
      my first car. I picked her up at the corner
because she never got her license, found her
      after school and drove home, top down
      on my rickety old convertible. She beat all
the video game levels I couldn't tackle, told me
      she knew exactly where her mom hid her
      presents, had to fake surprise every Christmas.

We stopped in the cemetery one gray day, stood
      surveying newer tombstones near the gate,
      older ones beyond the far hill. When the wind
became a gale, screaming in our ears, the rain
      cold and pointed as needles, we ran back down
      the winding path to the car. She hesitated, door
still open, found two quarters, placed them gently
      on the circular drive's worn concrete. *An offering,*
      she explained, as though this made sense, but
the wind died down, the rain settled to a calm drizzle,
      and she smiled at me. A good Christian girl,
      I should've seen her for a witch, stayed away
from the occult like my parents told me, but I was
      entranced, gleefully haunted by her pale
      blue eyes and the sky that hovered above,
threatened and blustered.

I didn't love her, but I could have, given an alternate
         world and time. I found out later she went
         to senior prom alone, when I didn't go at all,
and I thought we could have been each other's dates,
         could've taken photos together, could've been called
         gay (*derogatory*) by all our classmates, nothing
new for me and probably not for her. In ninth grade,
         a boy asked her to homecoming in front of me,
         and she said yes, hesitantly, and I should have
said, *Go with me. We don't have to be anything*
         to each other or to anyone. We can just be. But we
         were both too quiet, too less, and in the end all I had
to hold onto were her icy eyes and pale gold hair,
her smile when she gave the spirits a little token.

A Little Wild

I want:

    time to unwind itself, stop

        spinning me into a tomorrow

        with no footholds

    to feel what I felt when, ten years old,

        I roller-skated down the trail

        by my house, past a pond full

        of catfish, through green-lit woods

    hum of wheels on concrete

    buzz of insects in tall grass

    no helmet, no padding—skinned knee

        small price to pay for my arrogance

        if I raced down hills too fast

    a little reckless, a little wild, hungry

        for cloud-sketched skies, the way

        my skates rumbled over wooden

        slats on a makeshift bridge

    to lean over the railing at lake's edge

    to forget entirely I can't swim

Center

I dream only of one house—
my grandmother's. The blue carpet
      of her front porch, peeling
white paint on the railing. Chain-link
fence leaning into the alley.

You get one life, one center.
Base in a spontaneous game of tag
      the slide top where metal
burns or pinches, leaves a mark.
Flowers she tends until she can't.

A succession of dogs in black,
gray, brown, commandeer the same
      worn chair just outside
the entryway. Last chance to turn
around and pretend the key didn't fit.

Her body, her scent. Furniture
scattered to god knows where, a box
      of old magazines, zebras
striped with gold. Circle back each
night, find the holes in each chain.

Upon Learning of the Death of a Loved One by Suicide

spend at least 20 minutes sobbing somewhere
semi-private—a public restroom stall. your car
in a Starbucks parking lot. check your red eyes
in the mirror before you leave. avert your gaze
from anyone you pass. fake smile.

drive home, flipping frantically through radio
stations & static. shudder at a Tom Petty song.
switch the sound off & move through traffic
in silence. air will feel heavy, foggy even.
that's to be expected.

once alone, find the bathroom again—yours
this time. assume the position: back against
wall, knees bent, arms crossed, head down.
struggle for air. scream if no one's around.
or even if they are.

order a double cheeseburger. take three bites
before forgetting how to chew. field texts
from peripheral people who heard you're
shattered. wonder how they know. flash-
back to the morning, the quiet before.

get coffee with someone who knows. cry
even if she doesn't. accept the muted shock

of the barista sweeping the floor. dial
their number one last time. find sweet
agony in a voicemail.

wait for a letter, a knock on the door—
something left behind. receive only silence,
unknowing. catalog every detailed memory
in a word doc as it comes to you & then
delete it all.

attend a memorial. hold it together for
a while. ruin the sleeves of your sweater.
realize you dreamed these moments once.
eat Mexican food after with an appetite
you thought you'd lost.

dream about them for the first time. wake
sobbing for the first time. look askance
at everyone, wondering who will make
their exit next. always be afraid of losing
everything.

pass someone on a downtown street
who looks like them. lose their photo.
write three essays, a dozen poems, half
a novel about death. find their eyes
in strangers.

hold your best friend as she screamsobs
on her apartment staircase. resent her
for wanting to die. resent yourself
for feeling resentment. imagine another
funeral.

almost let the anniversary pass without
marker. almost forget. promise yourself
you'll visit. it's been too long. remember
there is no one there. swallow. sigh.
fall asleep. eventually.

dream of them again. wake before dawn,
staring at the ceiling. move on for a while
before returning to pick at the scab. laugh
now & then. lose others to other things.
cancer. age. drugs.

attend more funerals. stack your griefs.
consider burning the black dress
in the back of your closet. it will get worse.
everything does. but you're still here, &
though sometimes that feels like a fluke,
it's something.

Sting or No

I fell in love once / with a dark-haired boy / who played guitar / & was sometimes / a little bit / mean to me // eyes like the ocean on a cloudy day / a view I'd seen exactly once / but held onto / like I'd discovered it // I stubbed my toe / on that island beach // bought a postcard / to stick on my bedroom wall / pretend I'd seen more / of the world than a handful // my mother found a jellyfish / at water's edge / limp & still in the sand / probably dead / but maybe not // we couldn't tell, couldn't know // part of me wanted to touch / find out what that pale mass felt like / sting or no // instead I sat & watched waves / stumble in & out //

the boy with dark hair & blue eyes / finally told me / he'd always liked me / since the day we first met // words I'd spent a year longing for / dropped casually / only a month before he moved / a thousand miles away // he never kissed me / never even held my hand // his absence left craters // I saw the ocean again / the summer after he left // different beach / same water / glowering sky // sat on the boardwalk / with an ice cream cone // felt for a moment / as invincible as seventeen-year-olds / are meant to feel / wild & wanting / hungry beyond measure // I imagined packing my suitcase / creeping out of the hotel room / while my parents snored / building a life from scratch / failing to forget / the color of his eyes

And Now the Moon is Rust

Gray snow crushed against the curb.
An extinguished sparkler in a tin
bucket. I'm no good with endings.
We touched something cold and sharp
in each other, so maybe this is best.
A quiet exit. No lights ringing
the stage, no voices murmuring
in the back of a crowded bar.

We never did share a bottle of wine,
but you sipped my Long Island before
stepping into late October streets.
The claws of a cat ticking along
a windowsill. Your voice somewhere
between glitter and starlight. I take
nothing back, not a second. Close
my eyes and count, slowly, to seven.

I walked deep in caves where daylight
choked and died, thought of rockslides
and trapped miners, saw no difference
between the dark behind my eyelids
and the world around. But I heard
your laugh, the way it cut through
stagnant air. We slept on the living
room floor of someone else's apartment

and woke to stumble through the woods
like lost boys, strange and kindred.
We found something in spring,
resurrected in fall, and it lit the sky.

Ode to Missouri

there are no trees. view from a plane window,
brown and gray, distant rivers. an abstraction.
     snowless and ever-warm. sweet tea and southern
accents. stretches of flat plain. whitewashed fences.
farmland as far as the eye can see, pastures of cattle,
     silos breaking the blue. winding one-lane roads
through ugly countryside. no hills, no bluffs,
no scenery. in-between place, rest stop
     on the way to somewhere else. flat
non-accent of news anchors. front porches
     and tobacco stains, tractors in high school
     parking lots.

half-truths and rumors, a confusion of places
and movie sets, none of which are—
     my first shot of vodka in a sticky-floored
piano bar, fireworks over the roof of a house
     next door to the public library.
my first pair of in-line skates
on the cracked sidewalk, a hundred games
     of mini-golf, the deaths of grandparents
one by one. too many churches I've seen
inside of, too many hymns. houses I've lived
     in, the playground where I lost a tooth.
not home anymore maybe, but place of origin,
motherland. the old aunt whose car smelled

of smoke, who always sent me a card
full of cash on my birthday. sound of trains
passing in the night, graffitied freight cars
                rumbling along tracks older than all of us.

I may never return, but still—
                twenty-seven years is time enough to know
                she made me, birthed me, raised me, knocked me
                                down and spit me out and wiped blood
                from my scratched knees. I owe her something,
                a fondness at least, or rage. depends on the day
                                and weight of each memory. but
                I love her somehow, some way, stooped queen
of the midwest, doorway and anchor.

Wayward

Just echoes really. Ghosts etched in ash. The roof only half-existent,
wind chimes dangling from the blackened eave.

There was something here once, a voice rustling in creaking wood.
When he died, they took his eyes and burned the rest.

He had a black dog, restless and only half tame. For her, he left money
in a yellow envelope on the porch. Someone took her in.

Considering Cigarettes

I'd always been told not to, so I didn't. We talked for hours
about smoking in the basement before your eighteenth
birthday, on the same couch where, years later, your dad

would sip wine and gently mock you for a night when
you mixed too many drinks and ended up with a porcelain
crown. *How about a pipe?* you said, but that was too much

expense, more effort than a pack of cigarettes at the gas station,
too reminiscent of professors and old authors, dim offices
and books with cracked spines. When you finally turned

eighteen, I bought you a box of cigarettes made of chocolate,
a gift bag of lottery tickets and plastic knickknacks, a lei,
a coconut bra from the dollar store. You won two dollars

on the scratcher card. *Just once,* I said, but we never bought
any, although there was a convenience store down the street
and a Hy-Vee across the highway. We were in college then,

we were going to experience things, but were just two old women,
talking about literature and dead acquaintances. We forgot
about cigarettes, stumbled ahead while looking behind, marked
morose anniversaries with calls, then texts, then nothing at all.

Midwest Suburban

I forgot the way the world looks in daylight, the stark blue of the sky,
      trees burning green against its canvas. A bright green,
almost unnatural, like the lights framing the garage across the street.

I am not safe here. In sunlight, people stand in their yards, driveways,
      stoop on porches but don't lift a hand. In darkness, lit
cigarettes reveal faces beneath moth-adorned porchlights. Sometimes

they argue, voices low, snarling. I sleep surrounded by feral life.

My neighbors are old, attended by middle-aged women who come
      and go, packing up trash bags of aluminum cans to shove
in the recycling bin. A different car in the road every day, occasionally

edging into space I think of as mine. I drive close to the bumper, nearly
      striking it, scowling, as though they might see and fear
the helpless look in my green eyes.

II. PREACHER'S DAUGHTER

Baptism

You can drown in such
a small amount of water.
A bathtub, a puddle,
a creek swollen with rain.

Ghost Stories

I slept with the lights on, afraid
        to glimpse shadows of dead men
        stretching across the wall.
My mind populated my childhood
        bedroom with staring eyes, hunched
        figures, quiet shuffle of uncertain feet.

My father told me ghosts were just
        demons in disguise. My mother
        collected stories of the unexplained
like postage stamps. When he was out
        of town, I slept in her bed beside her, hushed
        and warm, as she told me of spirits
she'd glimpsed—faceless shades and gray
        figures cutting through the room. The smell
        of smoke when her sister died two hundred
miles away. Her father coming to her mother's
        bedroom window years after he was gone.

We lived two lives—one when he was home
        and one when he was away, different shows
and dinners, given over to our restless, eager
        hearts. Behind every word, every look
on my mother's face was that other self,
        the one she kept hidden. A ghost story
        all its own.

The Hand That Drowns

There's another layer of faith in baptism,

                  to believe you'll rise again from beneath

the water, trust the hand that drowns you

                  will also lift you up. I had no such faith

in second grade, although it was my father

                  who baptized me, his hands holding me,

hands that had cradled me, caught me,

                  clung to me since I entered this world.

The Sky Will Grow Dark for Days

Somewhere someone drinks blood
like wine. She says the world is tipping,
balanced on a knife edge, and when
will I realize I'm wrong about everything?

Her house is in order, although an absence
of dust is not the opposite of crumbling.
The dogs bark at every stranger who passes.
She calls me blind when I'm afraid
of how clearly I see. Taps her ear, lets the voices
kick in again, wiser, all-knowing. The flowers
against the house are dead, the mailbox
leaning like it's tired of standing.

Last year the condos across the street went up
in flames, but now it looks like no fire
ever touched them, like they've stood firm
and solid for decades, like there isn't mold
crowding the corners, water that crept in
when the roof was gone, when the gutted
rooms with their abandoned furniture stood
naked against the rain.

Dying Young

I used to imagine the Rapture, a sudden
disappearing, and how it would feel to stand
in an empty house while the world fell apart.

I never expected to live this long, grew up
swallowing stories of martyrdom and sacrifice,
waited to find one day a gun at my head.

Most Sunday mornings I wondered what
would happen if a shooter burst into
the sanctuary, debated whether I could

play dead on the floor beneath the pews.
If nothing else, it broke the monotony of hell
in a handbasket, shame and stuttering hymns.

Destined to die young, I knew, cut short
in my prime standing for something, even if
I didn't know just what. Now I stare down

a different barrel, the long years ahead,
and heaven and hell mean nothing to me,
distant nightmares from another time, cries
of fanatics who forgot their humanity
long ago.

Baptism II

I covered my nose
with both cupped hands
before he could finish
speaking, heard laughter
from below, noise from
a congregation I was far
too scared to look upon.

South of Easy

I know you don't want to hear from me,
        but I believe the grass was a different shade
        back then. Your eyes shone warm and bright,
and your laugh came so easy.

Yesterday I almost called you, thought about
        turning up prodigal on your doorstep,
        but I knew it wouldn't be a parable,
not even a heartwarming story.
        I'd come in and sit on the sofa,
        and you'd tell me how glad you are
that I finally came around.
        We wouldn't talk about the food
        you've stockpiled or your certainty
        that all the lights will go out at once,
leaving both of us in the dark.

This dance is old, and I'm tired of watching
        my steps, so here we are—a town apart,
        a canyon between us. I haven't told many
people about you. It's too hard to explain
        how we don't talk, our only contact
        the cryptic texts you send, thinking
yourself my savior, the messages I read
        and reread and finally ignore.
        I'm still waiting for you to show up

at my door, unrecognizable, thrusting your heart
        at me like a baby bird fallen from a tree.

        I do wish I could fix you, but I don't have
the tools, and anyway, you were supposed to be
        the caregiver here. Instead I learned a specific
        vocabulary, a strict code of conduct, and how
best to let you down easy. I know you think I'm crazy
        and detached, but I promise you: this is one
        cord I can't sever. I've just learned not to touch
it, to keep the vibrations from thrumming through me
        like an ache. But still, sometimes, they do.

To Be the Lamb

I have never asked my father if he would
sacrifice me to his god like Abraham, like Jephthah
did his nameless daughter, because I already
know the answer, and I don't need to hear it
spoken aloud.

Old-Fashioned Tent Revival

The girl sitting outside the revival
tent, long hair windblown in her face,
only here for the free meal offered
before the preacher starts talking.

That's how they get you, promise
fullness and leave you starving.
They make fun of the Catholics, priests
with white collars, confessional

like a secret room every weekend,
but ask you to get down on your knees
until they turn raw-red, cry out your sins
at every key change. Do not turn

back, don't look behind. Her face
under the white tent is holy, eyes
catching lights that stain the pastor
with sweat. Come as you are, he says,

but she has no other way to come,
dress too old and too short, knees
showing beneath worn cotton hem,
and maybe this will be enough, this

feeling in the moment of epiphany, music
becoming one with summer heat. Maybe
she will finally hear every word
she needs, and if she closes her eyes

and lifts her hands to the sky she can't see,
almost the noise sounds like God's voice.
Somebody's at least, bigger and broader
than any she's ever heard, and maybe

it will be enough, to take hold of this
salvation in the palm of a stranger's hand
and pretend it feels like love.

As You Wish

All turned to poison now. Dust would be better, easier

    to brush aside, but instead toxicity. Sickness. Disquiet.

I know she has shuttered storage of her own, things never

    to be regained. Sometimes I imagine she curses

my name. I close my eyes and hear her weeping. She stood

    in the driveway and cried when I drove to Iowa

for a week, like I would get lost somewhere in empty fields

    between this city and that one, just disappear

beneath flat blue sky. Every farewell was fatal and none

    more than this. No grasping hugs in the airport,

no box of food to carry home. I imagine the stories

    she will tell about me, the myths she will construct

board by board. Sometimes I don't think of her at all. I keep remembering her favorite Bible verse—rivers

in the desert, a path in the wilderness. Always seeking

blossoming fields, flowers without roots, an eye

with no storm surrounding.

Baptism III

Just let it be over, I thought, a child who never
learned to swim, not even all these years later.
I screwed my eyes shut and when he pushed me
down, I forgot his insistence that I bend my knees
to make the action easier, thought of nothing at all
except my own fear of the water, but I was small
and he managed, brought my full weight under.

Psalm from a Vessel

Lord, soften my sharp edges.

      Sand and scrape until no jagged splinters

      persist, no discoloration or whorls that run

      contrary to your holy grain.

Give me a new face—yours—

      with a mouth that speaks only scripture

      and eyes that glow with grace. Burn the ugly

      words from my tongue, the *shits* and *fucks* and

      especially the *goddamns*. Erase me completely,

      until I look in the mirror and see not my reflection

      but yours, hear not my voice but your sweet accents.

Take from me the taste of first love,

      the feral ecstasy of sex, the wild sorrow

      of my lost child. Strip from me the bad

      and the good, comedy and tragedy alike,

      until all I feel is you.

Make me transparent, oh Lord, thin

      as the glass vase that sits on the dining room table,

      a vessel for your reckless and violent beauty.

      And, dear Lord, when rough hands cause me

      to stumble and fall, in my shattering, in my sharp

      and ugly pieces on the ground, may the only color left

be yours.

Hollow Place

No stained glass, just threadbare carpet & stiff-backed pews. Warbling voices
       on Easter. Songs with words so familiar, I forget how ugly they sound,
how slowly they chip away at what remains of me.

Grape juice and chalky pale crackers—cheap version of blood & body,
       watered-down salvation. Knees bent at the altar, hands pressed
to your spine. Tell me once again I am redeemed.

Sunday school rooms with peeling paint & threadbare Bibles, sometimes
       a dusty piano sitting out of tune in the corner, a single window
to watch congregants slip through the doors.

I feel verses in my soul, words stuck in my throat, so close to holy, so far
       from sacred. Sin between my legs, meaning nestled in the space
above, a hole waiting to be filled.

Empty in every way that counts, trespasses unforgiven. Vessel for life
       but blaspheme to call myself creator. You will know, they said,
one day, but all I see is shabby set pieces,

lines from a script, memorized, twisted & beaten like metal to build
           a gate that creaks with every entrance & each scorned exit.

Specter

I dreamed my own death. My body washed up
on a glistening shore, nudged there by whales
      of black and white. Some part
of me watched from above, at distant remove,
as my mother claimed what was left of me,
      stumbled through a crowded megachurch
and pleaded with blank-eyed worshippers.
A pastor with dark hair and no feeling
      in his soul. My death inconvenient,
in the way of Sunday services and all
the tithes yet to be gathered in paper
      popcorn buckets.

Flashed forward in my own body again,
not dead somehow, people around me
      only mildly surprised by my resurrection.
My mother always off to the side of every
conversation, searching through her purse
      for hand sanitizer or fiddling with something
on her phone, never quite looking at me.
I didn't thank her for gathering my body
      and returning it to me, only sat beside her
in the passenger seat while she drove us
to a university building I've never seen,
      the traffic lights turned to streaks in the rain.

I'm failing biology, I said, although I'm thirty
and haven't gone to class in nearly a decade.

      She shrugged, checked the rearview mirror.
Her hands gripped the wheel, nails short
and clean. She didn't drop me off anywhere

      but stayed with me, as though she too felt
the heaviness in my limbs, saw again
the stillness of my form on that beach,

      whales breaking the water one at a time.

View from the Baptistry

Behind my closed eyes,
the light changed, white
and blue, shot through
with radiance, and I
could believe in heaven
then in a way I could
never now. This, finally,
would save me. When
the end comes, I won't
be afraid because, by
virtue of this act, I call
myself redeemed.

I Fall Asleep Thinking About Bones

The ones inside me, the ones in the ground. Halloween decorations,
        dangling abstractions. Dancing skeletons on TV commercials,
figures following me into dreams. Disney bones rattling, shaking

after midnight, watched in horror, fast-forwarded beyond. The way
        my joints pop and crack, subtle movements of each curled finger,
each step. Biology classrooms and anatomically incorrect animal skeletons

made of plastic. Spiders who have no bones by right, ears protruding
        to signify a cat, turning flesh and cartilage into solid matter.
My uncle shivering in the cemetery at the idea of cremation, of leaving

no body behind to rise in the great resurrection he's been promised.
        What about decay? The smell and horror of all our dead cracking
out of the earth, eyes gone, skin eaten away or hanging half off, true

apocalyptic zombie nightmare. Some of us just want to leave bones behind,
        folded neatly beneath stone markers, to say we were here, we lived.
Here we lie, and we are the graves. A sign you can't turn from, etched

into permanence, until rain and wind wear it away like century-old
        tombstones on the other side of the hill, names and dates, whatever
message left behind anyone's guess. Bones are anonymous, only a hint of age

and physical sex, no identifying features, no clues to our lusts and leisures,
        our true selves hidden somewhere in heart and mind and 21 grams.
I'd rather be a ghost. Give me spirit over osseous matter—I prefer

the intangible, my childhood bedfellow, my own personal haunting.
        When my bones return to dust, I like to think something will
        remain,
whispers of all I used to be.

Of the Body

In Baptist churches there is no rosary to cling to. Something

    to occupy hands, focus minds. We hold our anxieties

close in our chests, say prayers silently, choose our own

    rough words. Still I say *we* although I am not of *them*

anymore, standing on a different coast, wincing at the familiarity,

    songs that so casually drift through my head. Baptized

in one church, married in another, memorized verses,

    ate of the body, ran through back corridors, felt at home.

The hardest part of letting go is giving up that sense:

    it can be so easy to belong.

My uncle leading my fading grandmother through the sinner's prayer,

    my aunt smiling at a funeral because no farewell feels final

when you believe in forever. My father in tie and matching shirt my mother ironed for him the night before, studying

his scribbled sermon notes in handwriting I could

barely decipher. The billowing clean white robe he wore

for baptisms, water pulling the fabric out like flower petals caught

in gentle tide. Hush before each hymn, slow turning

of thin pages, so easy to rip and tear, pen marks of underlined

verses showing through. Fidgeting in new pantyhose,

a run down my back leg, shoe on the seat back in front of me,

gray scuff marring black. Coins my mother pressed

into my hand before the offering plate passed by, clink

of quarters that could have bought machine gum,

sent a bright pink orb twirling down into my waiting palm.

My old world, the one that raised me, sheltered me,

called me home, permanent and predictable, familiar

in its coldness, unending, unfailing, glory hallelujah amen.

To R

There is still a space we inhabit, apart
from everything else. Cobwebbed
and shadowed sometimes, boarded up,
haunted but never abandoned. Let's
revive dead languages, speak feral
tongues. Make smudged angels
of dust on the floor. Heart to heart,
finger pressed to finger, I owe you
more than a penny, more than a pound
of flesh. I'll buy you a hundred trinkets,
a thousand symbols of things I can't speak,
all these things that fall apart in the naming.
The same stuff we're made of, same stars
and slow circling sky, an even dozen,
a full spin of the zodiac apart.

Two Kinds

There are two kinds of preacher's daughters—
good girls and bad girls. I fell squarely

in the former category, straight-A student,
quiet and accommodating. I never went out,

so my parents forgot to give me a curfew
until I was seventeen and went to a late movie.

No cigarettes, no alcohol, no boy with his hands
running up my thigh, much as I wanted it,

wanted to feel desired, adored, seen.
Much as I wanted to feel anything at all.

I floated the high school corridors like a ghost,
sat the Sunday pews like a martyr. Didn't even

begin to wake up until I turned twenty, spent
another ten years cracking the lily-white veneer

of my angelic belief. These days, I don't hold
to anything my parents taught me, and my teen self

would be so ashamed to see what I've become.
Sweet girl, I love you, I'm sorry, but you can't begin

to imagine the freedom of heathens, the relief
when blasphemy loses its sting.

Antidote

Staggering expanse of night sky, the few
stars this close to town, sliver of moon above.

In the deep blue, the black drape, hangs
something holy—same thing I used to feel

murmuring inside me, sacred and wild.
Sanctuaries and stained glass, thin orange

carpet, pews with rigid spines leaving sore
spots in the middle of my back. My father

decrying the evils of this nation from his pulpit,
never specifying, rarely naming names. But

I knew the things he cursed in front
of the TV, words he muttered under

his breath. In his eyes I stand now
the worst kind of sinner—rejecter and stray,

damned by choice and bloody heart.
Maybe he tried to lie, to love through gritted

teeth, but I want the kind of love I learned
to feel—wide and unrelenting, without question.

Those buildings aren't for me, those stale rooms.
The night wind its own cathedral, the stars points

of pale light sharper than every window, wind
sweet enough I could almost forget the echo

of apocalyptic silence that tugs at my mind, inhale
starlight and exhale every drop of poison within.

Redeemed

He lifted me from the water, drenched through
the white gown and old clothes I wore beneath,
and I didn't mind the wet, the way my hair glued
to my face or the drops sliding down into my eyes,
didn't care even for the hundred-some gazes trained
on me, the clapping distant, muffled by the sound
of water sloshing in my ears. I was glad to be
through the trial, accepted, chosen, truly aware
and relieved, for the first time, to be alive.

To Dust

I heard the other day
      the moon is rusting, and god,
nothing is permanent, the whole
solar system tired. How long
      before the Milky Way turns
to dust? We lie awake long
after we should have been asleep,
      talking about whatever lies
after this life, and what if
it's nothing, after all.
      The only consolation
of religion the certainty
death is not the end. Even
      when we do part ways, we will
once again find each other, you and me.

I don't believe all that anymore,
      heaven and hell, a bland eternity.
Maybe this is it—these days
of quiet routine and minor annoyances,
      trash needing to be taken out, little
yellow birds pecking at flowers
in the yard. Isn't that enough? Sometimes
      this life is so painful, I can barely breathe,
and sometimes so beautiful
I don't want to close my eyes.

Last weekend, driving down a dark
country road, woods on either side,
we saw a baby fox scamper across the gravel
        and into the trees, a doe lift her head lazily
and gaze back at us through
the windshield. I fell asleep to frogs calling
        to each other in the creek, thinking
of love, your body beside mine,
reassuring in every slow, sleeping breath.
        Maybe this is all we have, this life,
and oh—how lucky we are.

New Religion

I have imagined leaving and being left.
Bags packed and shoved into the trunk

and backseat. A quiet that falls in a house
unused to absence. The dogs staring out

the window, studying each car that passes
and doesn't slow. To keep a name like a scar

or let it fade. To stack all the things that no
longer matter in neat boxes and escort them

to Goodwill. To be solely my own again.
I don't recognize the world without,

and I'm not sure I can learn the language.
But also: I don't want to be her, the reason

you grow sour with age instead of softer,
the reason you scream at God in whispers.

A god neither of us believes in these days,
but we return to nonetheless. Not in

sanctuaries or before altars, but in the unique
dark after midnight, the hush following

a long silence. Maybe he's punishing us still.
We don't believe, but these are the words

we know: sin and retribution, shame
and sorrow. Too old already to learn new

phrases, to understand that we can pray
to each other, our bodies the altar,
each touch a hymn.

III. ALMOST MOTHER

I Guess This Is Goodbye

You have shrunk my world
to the space between two fingers,
expanded it beyond galaxies.
I didn't know it was possible to feel
at once small and infinite, larger
than the sky, calmer than the height
of spring.

That's what I would have said if ever
we'd met, if ever you grasped my finger
with your entire hand. I wrote those words
a month ago, anticipating seeing your face,
imagining 3 a.m. with you and dim light
through the back window. I was ready to be
a poet again for you, to be anything
your racing heart required of me.

I don't know if there are words beyond these—
or worlds, for that matter. I don't know if
we'll ever meet again on some far-off golden
shore. All I know is these days have to be enough,
these moments of seeing you in every room
of every place I am, your hand in mine,
your voice a song I'll never learn.

My head is full of plans to fill the quiet,
to populate this void with daisies, but all this
could never erase you. These streets were meant
for your feet, not mine, and if I laugh extra hard
or drink a little too much or stand listening to rain
fall through the trees, know that I am thinking of you,
of the way you waved through the dark.

Loose Strings

Everything feels like a metaphor these days. The binding of the book

on my nightstand comes undone—frail, hair-like strings, almost

invisible, slipping loose. I pull one until it snaps and hangs past the spine,

ruptured, a thread to worry. Too heavy-handed if I made it up,

but reality isn't subtle sometimes. There's no artistry to it, just blunt imagery.

Blank walls and found photos and the way all the flowers are wind-

beaten off the backyard tree. It's only symbolism because my mind can

think of nothing else, turning the same thoughts over and over

until I have to reroute them, snap the lights off each time they flicker on

in that dark room. The door has no lock, but I can turn away

each time my feet drag me to the threshold. I can avert my gaze. I can sigh

and go in, but only so often, returning with red eyes and paler

face, feeling like tissue paper. One good rainfall, and I'm in pieces.

Do Not Talk to Me About Heaven

cramped, dark room, her body
fluttering above my head.

> still there, her hand seemed to wave.

fingers traced the swelling—
lungs, heart, feet, hands, head.

phrases circled—too far, too much,
too severe, no chance.

awake until four a.m. writing letters
> in the dark.

five months. hidden on a side street.
wish the darkness was total.

> emptiness stepping into
the silent hallway. a sudden chasm.

left town for two days, came home
> empty-handed.

bleeding, milk leaking, tears
in the shower, in bed, sitting on the floor
> in the corner, staring out

at blossoming pink flowers
in the backyard.

not a mother, that's the problem. new
        self built around this thing created
from nothing, made me sick
        and turned my thoughts and carved
a space in my heart to nestle into.

do not talk to me about heaven

sometimes smile and pretend as though
        there is anything on the other side
        of this, as though the old me
will suddenly stand up and take my life
        from my hands.

inside shrinking, shuddering, curled
into a position not unlike hers
the last time. dig a hole and slide
        into it. keep digging.
catapult bricks through windows,
        set buildings on fire, tear down
        walls
and scream.

December

A florist called before showing up at my door, leaving
        yellow and purple blooms that died a week later.
One missed the trash and still lies dried and faded
        on the garage floor. I've taken out the bins
so many times since but never picked it up, once found
        the car with a flat tire and felt the world ending
all over again. The spare stained my fingers like ink.

I glance back at March, at April—jagged line between
        winter and spring—and I don't know how
I carried on, bent almost broken. How days multiplied
        without collapsing. Everybody said it would feel
different. A chasm between then and now, before
        and after. But when she was gone, no one talked
about the abyss that opened—with her to without.
        Or they looked in my eyes and saw only a hand
slipping beneath the waves. Silence blistered, deafening.

I thought I wanted what everyone else wants and has,
        but now I want for nothing but peace. I think of
mountains and lakes, woods in a spilled hush, and I take
        these moments now, early evening dark, staring up
and trying to catch my breath. The cold cuts in a familiar way,
        neighbor's lights send a glow over both our houses,
and here I am, straining for open sky in a subdivision, hands
        shoved into pockets of the navy cardigan I keep
        shrugging on, listening still for a voice that never spoke.

Dear Elise

Two weeks ago, I saw a picture book
my mother bought for you, and part of me
crumpled to the floor right there. The rest
moved on, as though nothing had happened,
as though none of it mattered anymore.

In another world, some parallel universe,
you are almost five months old, dark-haired
and gray-eyed. Your laugh is a sound I know
well. The dogs have grown used to you,
your grasping hands and eager giggles,

and I don't feel the dissonance I feel now.
As though I live in two realities, torn
between them. That other woman,
that mother, she doesn't imagine a world
without you. Why would she? The stuff

of nightmares, wake her sweating,
grasping through the dark to rest a hand
on your chest, feel its gentle rise and fall.
But me, I lie awake most nights and think
about the world where you appeared, bloody

and screaming, ripping me open. Oh, what
an entrance, little one. To think I grew

you like a wildflower. I still press you against
me in dreams, the softness of your fingers,
your smell something familiar and foreign,

a song I've heard a hundred times but still
can't place. We never met, but I cling
to you, as though some part of me knows
this is a dream. This won't last. Hold tight
while you can. And when I wake, my arms

are empty, but I recall so clearly the feel
of your skin against mine, your wisps of hair
brushing my chin. Another goodnight,
another thin cord between this world
and that one. Your heart beats—

a goddamn drum, and I feel its rhythm
even now.

Fragments

Under the deepest, darkest sky,
I drive home. Only the stars
tacked across its bruise-blue
surface keep it from falling,
collapsing around me like a sheet
draped over a forgotten chair.

I would have loved you hard
and well, torn into your chest
and cradled your shivering heart.

Faint, twangy voices cut
into the college radio station
every few seconds, crying out
of static about love and loss
in a language too fragmented
to understand.

I would have been your keeper,
building walls of warm-colored
brick around your spent form.

Out the window of the rusted
white pickup just ahead, a man
flicks a still-lit cigarette, its embers
scattering violent orange across

the highway—the only color
in the night.

I would have pinned you in black
and white, in photographs, until
you saw the grace in your body.

Over the horizon a water tower
peeks, bulbous and pale-glowing,
a second, smoother moon—
no pockmarks, no shadows.
If a man set foot on its surface,
he left no print.

I would have let you scrawl
in the margins of my every page,
pen strokes and question marks.

The light from the dashboard
casts a wavering violet glow
on the windshield, and for a brief
moment, I see an aurora borealis
shimmering in the night sky,
and I am somewhere else.

I would have wrecked your mind,
left my things littered everywhere,
painted apologies across the walls.

This House

makes noises, creaking floors sound
with the thuds of footsteps, shifts

and stretching. Just settling, we say, just
showing its age. But this house is younger

than me. I wonder how I reveal my years,
dust lining my ribcage, groan of muscle

and bone. Perhaps my kneecaps
are haunted, crackling and popping

with every bend, ghosts playing jazz,
snapping transparent fingers. Cobwebs

in my head, sleeping bats in the rafters
of my skull. Maybe each step I take leaves

an invisible print, a watered-down echo,
and my noises join those of this house,

both quiet and loud, the ones in the day
easily dismissed, the ones at night sending

a persistent shiver down the spine.

Three and a Half Months After

I found a baby rabbit stranded by the back fence. I can't say how.
     The dogs sniffed curiously, and I thought back to when
the lab tossed naked bunnies in the air like toys.

I heard something near a squeak and ran outside. The noise was just
     a bird screaming as the sun fell in the sky, but
there *was* a baby rabbit, gray and frail. I thought it was dead until
     I looked closely, saw the gentle shudder of its body.

The mother stood in the yard against the dogs as long as she could,
     desperate, and finally slipped through the wooden gate.
She waited in the yard between our house and the neighbors'—still
     and watching.

I sent the dogs back inside and gently lifted the baby with a shovel.
     I didn't want to touch it, whether that's myth or fact,
that the mother would catch my scent and turn away. It tumbled
     across the black surface, waking and reaching out with tiny legs.
I carried it over to the gate, placed it on the other side of the fence.
     The mother watched, didn't move. I wanted to tell her
to come collect her child, it was unhurt and safe, but there was nothing
     I could do.

I left them there, ten feet apart, the baby sleeping helplessly in grass
     that needed to be mowed, the mother alert and patient.
I didn't return until after dark, shining my phone's flashlight until it drew

moths. They were both gone. I held that moment close, the feeling
of saving something. A small thing, sure, inconsequential even,
but I had done it, had stopped nature from its relentless course.

There would be other rabbits and other losses loud and quiet, but this day
I had given a mother back her child, and that was something.
I already knew what it was to lose, and maybe she did too, but I gave her
what I couldn't give myself and wished blessings upon her,
this wild animal that made a home of the space under our worn deck.

Storage Space

There's a box in the basement, & I've trained my eyes not to see it,

just as I've schooled my mind to close off feeling

when I begin to lose my breath. You forget breathing is an action

until it becomes a struggle. Night, everyone else asleep,

I wonder when I will feel like myself again before I remember

this is who I am now—bleached sky before storm, growing

rumble of thunder. A dizziness I can't quite shake. I don't have time

to sit on the cold bathroom floor & contemplate the dark,

but spiritually I live there. The fan & rush of the shower cover

gasping sobs. Turn both on at once & scream until

you feel emptied out, hollow. I packed all my visions of the future

in a box, my helpless little dreams—bookends & clothes

I never wore. Even sympathy cards I didn't want but couldn't bring myself to let slip into recycling. I'm not sentimental,

I tell myself. I so quickly throw things away. But everything related
to this cavern inside me went into that box, & it fit

perfectly, as though this empty container was left in the cool,

dark basement for a moment such as this. A time to bury

things, to hide them from myself. When I go down to fetch

the fall décor or Christmas ornaments, I won't look

at the stuffed box, its hazy plastic walls through which I

can make out things that once mattered. I won't think

of all the things I never learned, the quiet that keeps

me up at night. I'll flip off the switch. Close the door.

Remnants

We saw a dead bird on our walk
the other day. A blue jay once, now
a lump of blood and feathers.

There's something exhausting
about death, in all its permutations.
I never learned to accept it, only

to see the end as yet another
beginning, a land to be conquered.
I come, after all, from a long line

of thieves and murderers, more
focused on the glory of victory
than how it's seized.

My dog sniffed the dead bird
with curiosity, but I see every death
as tragedy. Every squirrel crushed

on the road, every deer corpse along
the highway, each silent ambulance
and plain obituary—I feel nothing

casual. I grew up running from death,
leaning all my weight into the hope
of forever, but these days eternity feels

far more terrifying than quiet. The next day,
the bird was gone. Stolen by a stray cat
or cleaned up by the caretaker

in his red truck, who knows. Only a spot
of blood remained, dried and nearly blended

into the concrete.

Cicadas

I imagined these days
differently. Nights too.
Days where I wouldn't
have to fill the hours
because there would
never be enough, your
cries and laughter filling
every corner, rattling
the dust.

Instead it's quiet, sipping
coffee on the sofa, listening
to cicadas scream in the trees.
They're ugly things, too big
and too loud. I find their husks
everywhere, caught
on the railing of the deck,
hanging on the wood
like something alive, lying
in wait.

The dogs poke at dead ones
on our morning walks. What
would they do if that monstrous
thing suddenly took flight?

I don't sit outside. I suppose
I'm waiting for fall, for everything
to die and the air to turn cold.
One day the trees will be quiet
again, and in that hush I'm not
sure what sounds will echo.

Some Nights

We could have had a grave. A stone marker. An urn.
        Ashes were all anyone could promise.
I keep thinking of a tattoo, but my mind can't form
        an image, just her name like a brand, etched into skin.

Instead I asked for nothing. Afraid of the tangible,
        remains crowded in a box sitting
on the dining room table, waiting for me to do something
        signifying closure. I would have chosen
too quickly, scattered ashes to the wind, or else hidden
        them in the basement with everything else, nestled
deep in a corner where I couldn't see them unless I looked,
        unless I wanted to press my finger to the bruise.

Some nights I lie awake and imagine her in the next room.
        She'll wake any minute, and I will go to her,
even though I've yet to fall asleep and dawn is uncomfortably
        near. I will speak to her in a voice only she summoned,
tones I didn't know I possessed. The words won't matter
        for once. The night has lost its darkness, and instead
there's a faint glow around everything. Luminescence. Borrowed glory.

Cruelest Month

March never knows what she wants to be, caught
between bare bones of winter and spring's pastel
promise. Mostly she settles for cold without
beauty, a barren whistling. Counting the days until
the first red-breasted robin makes his appearance,
bouncing along the ground on stick legs.

Waiting rooms and the cold quiet of growing
uncertainty. That's what March has become
to me, hopeful glow transfigured into silver
that burns the skin. (April is no better, but we
don't talk about her, turn away every time
she bursts into the conversation.) March is all
lingering shivers and gray rain. Sunny days
that trick you into expecting warmth and laugh
when the wind cuts your face.

But even in that bedraggled end of winter,
in its persistence, pale pink blossoms feel
not so far off. Ask the fox curled into an infinite
circle, nose nestled beneath the duster of her tail.
Black feet tucked under her, eyes shut tight
against the dark. In the orange dawn light
she will wake, stretch the length of her body, claws
reaching toward earth, tilt her ears to bird calls,
faint breath of coming spring. Flint in her eyes

strikes into flame, sending her darting through dappled shade, well on her way into tomorrow.

Colors

The thing about grief
is it's more than gray.
More than raindrops
sliding down the glass
of the bedroom window,
more than the white
noise whir of the fan
as it oscillates.

There are dreams where he walks by me
down a florescent-lit corridor, moments
where he calls my name in greeting,
in passing. There's the feeling of her fingers
curled around mine, so real I can almost
believe I really felt it, didn't just imagine
the way her soft skin might feel.

Loss is more than
lying on the sofa
on a Saturday
afternoon, staring
at carpet that needs
to be vacuumed,
studying dust gathered
around the television.

Don't get me wrong, it's that too. But also—
the red flush of anger, the blue of forgetting,
the lavender of faded faith. It's all the jokes
no one else understands, movie lines
that are part of a lexicon I hold pressed
to my chest like a child gripping a book
in the library. Sometimes the missing burns
white and blinding, sun on snow. And
sometimes it's dark, no streetlights,
just the quiet murmur of the highway
in the distance and a dog barking
somewhere, woken, perhaps, by another
unquiet exit.

Every Time I Hear the Word Abortion

I don't immediately think of mine, but of each syllable
whispered & sneered, thrust out of downturned mouths
like phlegm, like a bug caught, spat out onto the ground.
My father's rage, transformation of my mother's face.
The old man standing with a sign outside the clinic.

The ultrasound my sister-in-law gave me at 11 weeks,
inside the cozy little Christian pregnancy center, dangling
modern light fixtures & purple walls, my guilt at being there,
at taking her up on the offer, but ultrasounds aren't cheap.

The feeling of sin, a spreading pool of ink, even at 29,
even when I didn't believe in those transgressions anymore.
Call it brain rot, my thoughts washed in the blood of the lamb,
red seeping into every gray cell. A secret, a curse, unforgivable,
unthinkable. The mind lets go but never really forgets.

I don't want to argue or defend, don't want to give testimony,
to talk about fear & relief, rising panic that had me texting
my mother in a way I never had before, even though I feared
to tell her the truth, sheltered in the twists of a lie.

The way I didn't sleep the night before, poised on a knife edge
of pain. How long it took me to feel comfortable even hearing
the word, seeing it casually slide across my phone screen.

How even now I want to turn away from the curve of the *a*,
sharp point of the *b*, gaping black hole of each *o*.

The people who stopped speaking to me, friends who disappeared.
How my father sees me as selfish, murderous, broken, when
I have never felt more holy, more whole. The way I feel—tired,
angry, & so, so sad. Powerless. Watching a car crash
in slow-motion, losing control of the wheel in a dream,
the highway thickening, unspooling like gray ribbon beneath me.

The silence I kept for so long, the fear of being disowned,
scorned, hurt when I already hurt so much. The eggshells
I walked on in slippered feet, the words I didn't dare open
my mouth to speak.

Mother Viper

Autumn shrugs into view, closer
skies. A slow and gentle dying.
Stacks of Halloween decorations
piled in the basement, probably
cobwebbed for real now. I
should have bought costumes.
I should be sleepless—and I am
sometimes, just not in the way
I anticipated. Too many nights,
I stumble toward unconsciousness
and feel afraid, jolt myself awake
in panic because I remember
too well the feeling of a body
that no longer feels familiar.

It's rained all week, and normally
I love the gray, the patter of drops
against the aluminum siding,
the way they echo like a song
in the fireplace. But these days,
the sky feels too heavy, air
too thick. I could suffocate on it,
and the thought is deep and old,
yanks me back to second grade
and a baptism I didn't want,
the water swallowing the light,

a crowd of people below clapping
and me pressing my nose closed
with the desperation of the dying.

I don't have it in me to tell anyone
there is no next time. I can't walk
that road again, feel my body drift
away, feel another body torn
from mine, swollen and already gone.
There is no cure. I'll let my days
waste away, every poem touching
the same bruise, pressing it.
What is left but this? Who am I
but this—wrecked, weary,
venomous as the day is long.
I should be golden-eyed and wild,
curled in wait. Instead I watch the world
pass, bare fangs at my own reflection.

Interloper

I caught a wasp this morning, pinned between
a plastic drinking glass and a napkin, carried her
outside like a prisoner, like a queen. It's funny,

I'm really not that person. Insects that make it
into the house don't usually make it out, especially
if they have stingers. But something about her

crawling every inch of the kitchen window,
seeking a crack to set her free, made me catch

and release. Eventually, the cat would have
killed her, toyed with her maybe, ripped
wings and legs off one by one. I let her go,

set the upside-down glass on the patio table,
tipped it over and darted back inside, gave her
a chance to flee without seeking revenge.

Slid the glass into the dishwasher, napkin
into the trash. The window is clean,

a clear view of deep purple flowers on the tree
beside the deck, and I could understand her
confusion, how the world she knew seemed so close

yet she couldn't find her way back to it, the pane
a near-invisible obstacle, meeting every desperate stab
with firm resistance. I'm not old, but I'm getting

sentimental with age, I think, crying at the ends
of romance novels and fumbling with gentler feelings.

I used to think myself above everything, and now
I just want to be in the thick of it all, the corny and trite,
the unoriginal. We repeat the same words because

they're true. We hold hands because the feeling
never gets old. If it does, heaven help me. Or hell
or whatever nothing lies beyond. Prayers were part

of the former me, but the farther I get from faith,
the closer I feel to everything.

Memorial

Last spring the neighbor came over and helped us weed the flowers in the front yard, restoring this little garden we never wanted to its former glory. As we ripped dead stalks from the dirt, she talked about the child she'd lost, the quiet that comes afterward, the joy of her youngest son. I wanted to thank her——for trying to give me hope in a spring that felt colder than winter, for giving me an excuse to use my fingers, which had forgotten how to do much of anything but press crescent moons into my palms. I recalled that our garden once belonged to her best friend who had died months before, that this unasked-for weeding was an act of remembrance. Every breath we take, every movement just an echo of someone who can no longer speak. We filled three giant brown bags with gray stems and thorny twigs, intruders and plants never meant to survive the weight of snow. She waved goodbye and walked back to her house, and I sat down on the step outside the front door, felt the dirt pressed between my fingers and the playful late spring breeze. Every thought, every dream an echo, lest we forget.

Salvage

The character I relate most to in Muppet history
       is the old woman in *Labyrinth*, decades
of possessions piled on her back, weighing
       her down, serving as home and restless anchor.

Stumbling through a junkyard wasteland, piles
       and pieces, scattered memories, broken picture
frames, cracked gray cubicle walls and window
       screens slashed by cat claws, stripped and worn.

Too often, the past feels like something I carry,
       places I've known and felt in my core—park
by a goose-swarmed lake, little blue house,
       Baptist church, its steeple the tallest thing

in a one-horse town. All these broke down years
       ago, and things will certainly keep breaking—
loves and smiles, promises whispered before
       a clutching selfie, bones that seemed set and firm,

turned out instead fragile. I used to try to stitch
       each one up, desperately, but thread only lasts
so long, is so easily pulled loose again. Study
       my face in the mirror, compare it to old photos.

The resemblance is uncanny but hardly there.

      I know her no longer, know her better than anyone,
the self I divided into uneven pieces—a shard

        for parents, this friend, that one, my childish need

to belong. I had to create a self for me from leftovers,

      things I could scrounge together from that junkyard,
a gold ring in the clearance bin, a pair of boots

        snatched from the rack. Sometimes it's easier—

better, actually—to let things fall apart, and find

      in the deterioration, the rebuilding, finally, peace.
My shoulders aren't bent under that weight

        anymore, and I think I might live elsewhere

than in this labyrinth, beyond oubliettes and cracked
doorways, as myself, as her—the woman I so wanted to be.

Weightless

I'm not ready to be all right, soft & easy-smiling, come what may.
        The weight of falling asleep weightless, of finding dreams
unsettling when they mirror a world I forgot: fretting & wrung
                hands, sweat-dampened fingers, neglected books, clocks tick
at double speed. I wake up, fumble for daylight, the dog at my feet,
        her steady breath like a sigh.

I like best the nights when I forget my dreams, when hours pass in gray
                haze that slips away on waking. One half of my brain digs
for pain I can't feel, the other shushes & soothes, presses a hand
        over her mouth to stifle any words that sting. *Just be*, she says,
just accept feeling okay.

But as a teen, I imagined trauma like shimmering gloss, ghosts
        & oracles, standing on a river cliff, telling everyone some truth
in words they wouldn't understand. I never felt all right, only lost.
        I gave a dull sheen to the feeling, just to keep myself alive,
just to pretend I gathered flowers instead of weeds.

An older woman once told me there's nothing wrong with a simple life.
        I smiled & didn't believe her, but these days I think often
of the waffles she made each Friday morning, strawberries in a bowl
        on the kitchen table, her quiet delight, & I repeat her words.
To myself, to everyone. *Isn't this enough?* Take your daisies, your fallen
        leaves. Let the course plot itself.

A Kind of Blasphemy

to miss her / grieve her / but still feel free // to know / I don't want new titles / scrubbed-over portraits // to sit in the quiet of a room / that should have been taken / from me // to carefully order books on the shelves / trinkets with colors that caught my eye // to study women / who walk down the street / pushing strollers / trailed by toddlers // to feel at once / kinship & divide // to celebrate with friends / stand in stores / pick out tiny clothing printed with animals / fold it neatly into a gift bag / pretend it all means nothing to me //

loss & gain / sorrow that broke me / relief that sustains me // how do you say / *I loved her* / & also / *I love this life* / in one breath // to hurt & laugh // to let pain scab over / fade to an off-color scar // something to explain away / years down the line / oh, this? / I grew a person / but imperfectly / had to remove the remains / like a cancer // I'm fine now / more or less / just a few pangs / here & there / just a shadow / of the thing itself //

sometimes I close my eyes / peek into the world / where we live / she & I both // most days / I avoid thinking / about what could have been / because I love what is // I would have worshipped her / with every inch / of my skin / every breath a prayer // I still do // but also / I don't need to repent / my empty womb / my choice / how easily the years may pass // cigarette in a sanctuary / curses in a chapel // this is just another step / of my sacrilege // another quiet letting go.

Notes

The line "the moon held water" in "June Burial" is a colloquialism for a crescent moon. I first heard it from an older woman who had lived in Missouri her entire life, and it has never left my head.

The images in the first stanza of "Ode to Missouri" are almost all actual things I have heard people say about Missouri since moving to Maryland.

"Old-Fashioned Tent Revival" is heavily inspired by the music of Ethel Cain.

The Bible verse referenced in "As You Wish" is Isaiah 43:19. Several of the lines come from actual text messages from my mother.

The line "Here we lie, and we are the graves" in "I Fall Asleep Thinking About Bones" is adapted from a similar line in *Harrow the Ninth* by Tamsyn Muir. "I'd rather be a ghost" is a reference to a song of the same name by Semler.

Acknowledgements

My endless gratitude to the editors and staff of the journals where versions of these poems first appeared:

Capsule Stories: "I Guess This Is Goodbye" and "Loose Strings"

Glass Mountain: "Upon Learning of the Death of a Loved One by Suicide"

indicia: "Ode to Missouri"

Kissing Dynamite: "Three and a Half Months After"

Last Leaves: "Dying Young" and "Two Kinds"

Levee Magazine: "Wayward"

Ligeia Magazine: "Mother Viper"

The Meadow: "And Now the Moon Is Rust" and "The Sky Will Grow Dark for Days"

Mud Season Review: "Fragments"

Near Window: "Echoes"

Night Music Journal: "Cicadas" and "Midwest Suburban"

Parentheses Journal: "Colors"

Phantom Kangaroo: "Ghost Stories"

Ripe Literary Journal: "New Religion"

Tabula Rasa Review: "Considering Cigarettes" and "Old-Fashioned Tent Revival"

Thimble Literary Magazine: "Hollow Place"

A Thin Slice of Anxiety: "Do Not Talk to Me About Heaven," "Interloper," and "Remnants"

Words & Whispers: "This House"

This book and these poems would not exist without the support and kindness of all the amazing teachers and professors I've had the privilege to work with, both growing up in public school and in my time in the creative writing program at Lincoln University. I especially want to thank Greg Brownderville and Elijah Burrell who both helped me strengthen and grow my poetry and helped me find my own voice as a poet. As corny as that may sound, it's very true.

Another big heap of gratitude goes to my community of friends who are my family, who endlessly support me, even when we live hundreds of miles apart. Naming all of you would take too long, but you know who you are. I see your likes and hearts and comments on every poetry post, and every single one means so much to me. I'm so lucky to have so many amazing, loving people in my life.

And finally, Josh, thank you for being the only thing about which I'm completely certain.

About the *Author*

Savannah Cooper (she/her) is a Pushcart Prize nominated poet, self-taught photographer, and bisexual mess. Her work has been previously published in more than 40 journals, including *Midwestern Gothic, Mud Season Review,* and *Parentheses Journal.* She holds a BA in English with an emphasis in Creative Writing from Lincoln University of Missouri and currently resides in Western Maryland.

About the Press

Unsolicited Press is based out of Portland, Oregon and focuses on the works of the unsung and underrepresented. As a womxn-owned, all-volunteer small publisher that doesn't worry about profits as much as championing exceptional literature, we have the privilege of partnering with authors skirting the fringes of the lit world. We've worked with emerging and award-winning authors such as Amy Shimshon-Santo, Brook Bhagat, Elisa Carlsen, Tara Stillions Whitehead, and Robyn Leigh Lear.

Learn more at unsolicitedpress.com. Find us on Instagram, X, Facebook, Pinterest, Bsky, Threads, YouTube, and LinkedIn. Unsolicited Press also writes a snarky newsletter on Substack.